# African Beginnings

# AFRICAN BEGINNINGS

JAMES HASKINS & KATHLEEN BENSON

PAINTINGS BY FLOYD COOPER

LOTHROP, LEE & SHEPARD BOOKS · MORROW

NEW YORK

ISBN 0-688-10256-5 (trade)—ISBN 0-688-10257-3 (library)

I. Africa—History—Juvenile literature.   [I. Africa—History.]   I. Benson, Kathleen. II. Cooper, Floyd, ill. III. Title.

DT22.H323 1998   960-dc20   94-9848   CIP AC


With special thanks to Dr. John Henrik Clarke and Dr. Enid Schildkrout for their invaluable assistance.

# CONTENTS

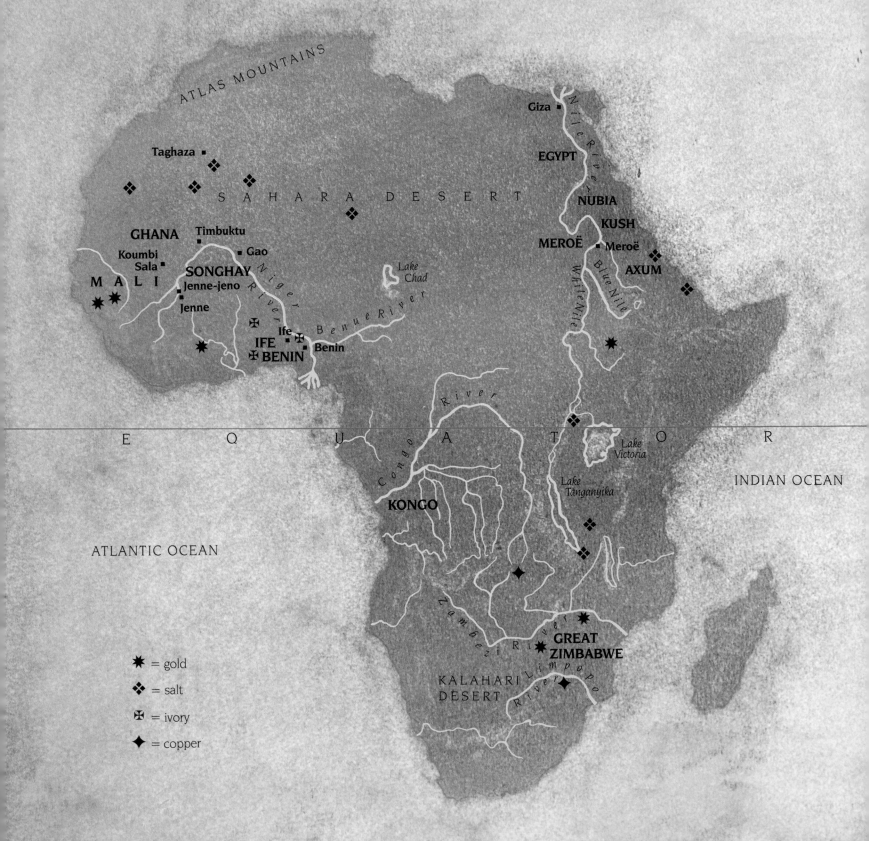

# Ancient Africa

ATLAS MOUNTAINS

Giza ■

Taghaza ■

EGYPT

S A H A R A    D E S E R T

NUBIA

KUSH

GHANA    Timbuktu

MEROË    Meroë ■

Koumbi
Sala ■

Gao ■

AXUM

SONGHAY

M A L I

Jenne-jeno ■

Jenne ■

Ife ■

IFE

Benin ■

BENIN

Niger River

Benue River

Lake
Chad

White Nile

Blue Nile

Nile River

E        Q        U        A        T        O        R

Congo River

Lake
Victoria

INDIAN OCEAN

Lake
Tanganyika

ATLANTIC OCEAN

KONGO

Zambezi River

GREAT
ZIMBABWE

KALAHARI
DESERT

Limpopo River

✴ = gold

✤ = salt

✠ = ivory

◆ = copper

This map shows the general locations of the most important ancient African kingdoms and
cities, which rose and fell in the period from 3800 B.C. to A.D. 1800. Territory and power ranged
over time, with one empire often taking over another.

AFRICAN CIVILIZATION DATES BACK TO A TIME (BETWEEN TWELVE THOUSAND AND SEVEN thousand years ago) when the region called the Sahara—now a vast desert—was green and fertile. Shepherds and herdsmen of the Sahara and southern Africa developed advanced herding and agricultural methods that allowed them to live at more than a subsistence level. Some people became skilled in crafts, such as pottery. Others created rock art. Activities portrayed in rock art made some six thousand years ago—including fishing, hunting, and gathering—reflect the lives of the people in these communities. Tools of stone, bone, and wood also give insight into their lives. As the people prospered, they began to engage in trade with their neighbors, and some communities grew in size and power.

Many cultures thrived on this huge continent, from the ancient kingdoms of Egypt and Nubia to the great sub-Saharan (south of the Sahara) empires in what is now western Sudan to the forest kingdoms of central Africa. As the Sahara became dry, the northern and southern parts of the continent were divided by an arid region larger than the mainland of the United States. A community that lived by farming in the Nile River delta developed a way of life very different from that of a nomadic people who lived near the Sahara Desert or a society that mined gold, silver, or copper. But through trade and other forms of contact, these societies influenced one another. As with all civilizations, the development of African civilization did not proceed along a straight line, but in a much more complicated fashion, with various kingdoms growing out of one another, centers of invention existing in different places at the same time, and many more communities flourishing than can be reflected in this book.

Although writing existed in several of the ancient kingdoms, African history was generally based in spoken tradition. But art, architecture, and artifacts have provided us with some important clues about how people farmed and prepared food, worshiped, organized governments, developed natural resources, made scientific inquiries and calculations, and much more.

Much of Africa's past was ignored or misunderstood by the Europeans who arrived in the 1400s in search of trade routes to India. Their search led them to the treasures of Africa, and it was these treasures, not Africa's rich history, that occupied their minds. At first, these traders sought gold, ivory, and spices. Later, after European colonization in the New World of the Americas, European traders undertook a huge commerce in human lives. To exploit the riches of the New World, they purchased millions of Africans, forcing them to leave their families and homelands forever. The slaves who survived the brutal journey to the New World brought a legacy of African history and culture as rich and diverse as the continent itself.

Many clues to Africa's past are still waiting to be discovered, explored, and better understood. Although this book can show only a glimpse of Africa's fascinating history, it is a place to begin.

# NUBIA

ONE OF THE OLDEST AND WEALTHIEST OF ANCIENT AFRICAN CULTURES was Nubia, south of the Egyptian kingdom, in the area of present-day southern Egypt and northern Sudan. The Nubian culture, which began around 3800 B.C., had plentiful resources and used advanced farming methods. Nubia carried on a thriving business in gold (*nub* was the word for "gold" in Old Egyptian), ebony, cattle, ivory, ostrich plumes, and more. Egypt was Nubia's major trading partner, in both materials and ideas.

Many archaeologists argue that the idea of divine kingship (the belief that a ruler is a god in human form) originated in Nubia, even before it appeared in Egypt around 3100 B.C. The Nubians created elaborate tombs with many chambers for their kings. These great mounds of gravel were filled with whatever the dead might need in the afterlife—incense burners, mirrors, inscribed plaques, and magical figurines to serve them.

# EGYPT

MUCH MORE IS KNOWN ABOUT THE ANCIENT CULTURE OF EGYPT. THE FERTILE SOIL AROUND THE GREAT Nile River—the longest river in the world—was ideal for farming, and farming fostered the development of early civilization. By 3500 B.C., the Egyptians had formed states. Four hundred years later, Lower and Upper Egypt were unified, and a great civilization began. Around 3000 B.C., the Egyptians developed a system of writing (in symbols called hieroglyphs), enabling them to record their history and share their knowledge with one another.

Egypt is best known to us as the land of the pharaohs (divine kings) and of the huge pyramids that were built as their tombs. In about 2550 B.C., the pharaoh Khufu (Cheops) ordered the building of the Great Pyramid at Giza, one of the largest structures ever built. The set of solid limestone blocks covers thirteen acres, and the base is a square, seven hundred fifty-six feet on each side. It may have taken ten years to build the access roads for the pyramid's construction and the underground burial chambers below the base, then another twenty years to build the pyramid itself.

Stones for the body of the pyramid were quarried at Jebel Mokattam, which is in present-day Cairo. The facing stones were brought from the southeast, near present-day Aswân. The massive stones were dragged to the Nile and carried by barges to Giza; then, with levers and ramps, they were transported uphill to the pyramid site. Thousands of laborers worked on the construction every day.

The Egyptians constructed about seventy pyramids over fifteen hundred years. The Great Pyramid was the tallest ever built. Such enormous projects required extensive engineering, construction, mathematical, and administrative skills.

Even tombs as large as the pyramids, however, could not prevent the decay of the bodies buried within them. So Egyptian scientists put their minds to discovering a method of preservation. Between 2500 and 2000 B.C., they invented the mummification process: a way of preserving dead bodies by treating them with special chemicals and wrapping them in layers of cloth.

11

Egyptians sailed the Nile River on trading expeditions. Carrying incense, ebony, grain, and ivory, they traveled south to exchange their goods for gold and slaves. In this way, they traded with the Nubians, as well as with the people of the kingdom of Kush, south of Nubia. The Egyptians later brought the Nubians and the Kushites under their control, but eventually they were taken over themselves for a century by the Kushites.

The mighty Nile was not only a remarkable trade route and a spur to civilization, it was also the source of Egypt's agricultural strength. Its annual flooding was critically important for farming. In order to calculate when to expect the floods, Egyptians studied the sun, moon, and stars, and in the process developed the world's first known twelve-month calendar of three hundred sixty-five days.

# KUSH AND MEROË

SOUTH OF NUBIA AND EGYPT WAS THE KINGDOM of Kush, a very old civilization that enjoyed a resurgence beginning around 900 B.C. For nearly a century, from about 750 B.C., the Kushite kings ruled Egypt. These kings are shown in Egyptian temple and tomb depictions as black pharaohs. The Kushite reign ended when Assyrian armies conquered Egypt. From the sixth century B.C. onward, the Kushite kings ruled their territory from the population center of Meroë, farther down the Nile.

Ruled by goddess-queens and god-kings, Meroë became a powerful empire by 100 B.C. It was renowned as an industrial center where local ore was mined, smelted, and forged into iron. The Meroitic culture may have helped to spread iron technology to other parts of Africa. The Kushites in Meroë developed their own system of writing, which has yet to be deciphered by modern scholars.

The Kushites traveled widely, and their civilization at Meroë was known for its distinctive art, architecture, and sense of enterprise. Even their use of animals was unusual: They domesticated elephants for military use and for impressive display.

Meroë eventually was overshadowed by Axum, its nearest neighbor. By A.D. 350, Meroë was part of the Axumite Empire, which covered what is now northern Ethiopia.

# JENNE-JENO

IN THE INLAND DELTA REGION of the present-day Republic of Mali in West Africa, the first known city south of the Sahara arose in a fertile land where the Bani and Niger Rivers flow. Jenne-jeno was an urban center whose advanced culture was marked by productive agriculture, elegant craftsmanship, and far-reaching trade. Established—probably by herders and fishermen—as a small group of round mud huts around 250 B.C., by A.D. 800 Jenne-jeno was a cosmopolitan center of some ten thousand people, surrounded by a massive mud-brick wall some ten feet wide and thirteen or more feet in height.

The people of Jenne-jeno traded first with the Timbuktu region downriver and later, by caravan, with North Africa. In exchange for Saharan salt and copper and Mediterranean glass beads, the merchants of Jenne-jeno offered an abundance of crafts, including gold and copper jewelry, as well as such agricultural produce as red rice, onions, and chili peppers. The oldest gold earring yet found in West Africa was found in excavations at Jenne-jeno, along with pottery burial urns and toys in the shape of animals.

Around A.D. 1400, Jenne-jeno was abandoned, and in the centuries since, oral histories relating to it disappeared, leaving the reason for its abandonment a mystery. A new city named Jenne arose about two miles away. It grew and prospered as a rich center for agricultural exports, and continues as such today.

# THE SPREAD OF ISLAM

NORTH AFRICAN ARABS traveled south to trade. They first sailed down the eastern coast of the continent, and by the seventh century they had begun crossing the vast Sahara Desert with caravans of camels to trade for African gold, silver, copper, ivory, pepper, kola nuts, salt, and slaves. In exchange, they brought spearheads and axes, glass, wine, and wheat. They also brought their religion, Islam.

Founded by Muhammad (who lived from about A.D. 570 to 632), the religion of Islam is based on the belief in one God, Allah, and on a life of devotion to Allah by the faithful. One of the most important duties of a Muslim, a believer in Islam, is to spread the faith, and Arabs went southward in ever-increasing numbers to settle in the African population centers and bring Islam to the people there. The religion of Islam allows for great diversity, so it was possible for Africans to adopt Islam and still keep many of their traditional ways.

The Arabs introduced not only their religion but also their systems of currency and credit, their administrative structure, their political ideas, and their language and writing. Many accounts of African history were written in Arabic script.

# GHANA

WHEN GREAT NUMBERS OF ARAB CAMEL CARAVANS STARTED TO CROSS THE SAHARA to trade, the West African kingdom of Ghana began to strengthen its power. Founded in the fifth century A.D., Ghana soon established itself as a center of the iron industry. When the trans-Saharan trade began to flourish, so too did Ghana, by taxing and monitoring the trade. Gold arrived from secret locations in the south, and between about A.D. 450 and 1230, more gold was traded in Ghana than anywhere else in the world. Salt—a vital commodity as a food preservative—came from the north, chiefly from the mines at Taghaza, in the Sahara.

The people of the original kingdom, the Soninkes, spoke the Mande language. In Mande, *ghana* means "warrior king," and the Soninkes were true to the name. They took over other kingdoms, and Ghana became an empire that covered most of the territory between the Niger River and the Atlantic Ocean.

At its height, in A.D. 1060, the empire influenced the territory of present-day Senegal, Mauritania, and Mali. Arab travelers described an imperial army of two hundred thousand soldiers, including forty thousand archers. Since many diverse cultures were incorporated into Ghana, the chief ruler had to have a strong system of justice and administration to keep peace in the empire.

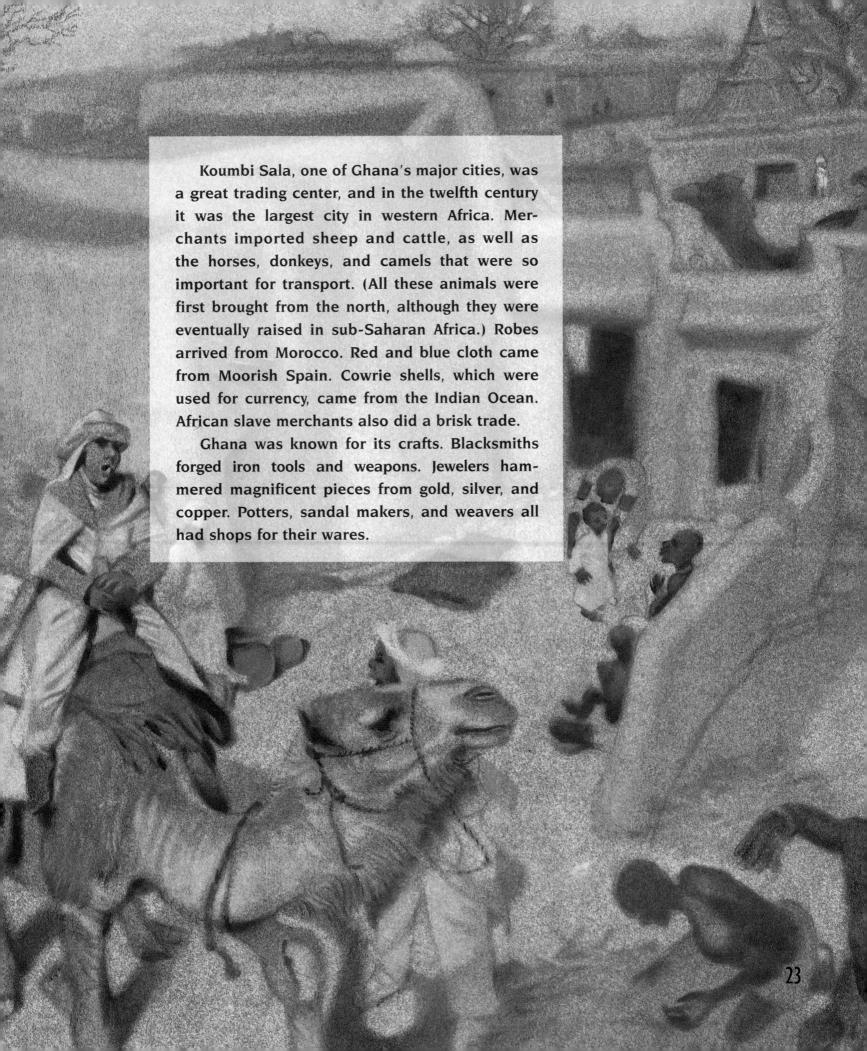

Koumbi Sala, one of Ghana's major cities, was a great trading center, and in the twelfth century it was the largest city in western Africa. Merchants imported sheep and cattle, as well as the horses, donkeys, and camels that were so important for transport. (All these animals were first brought from the north, although they were eventually raised in sub-Saharan Africa.) Robes arrived from Morocco. Red and blue cloth came from Moorish Spain. Cowrie shells, which were used for currency, came from the Indian Ocean. African slave merchants also did a brisk trade.

Ghana was known for its crafts. Blacksmiths forged iron tools and weapons. Jewelers hammered magnificent pieces from gold, silver, and copper. Potters, sandal makers, and weavers all had shops for their wares.

# MALI

IN THE THIRTEENTH CENTURY A.D., THE MANDINKA PEOPLE OF THE STATE of Kangaba emerged as successors to the Ghanaian rulers. Their Islamic emperor, Mansa Musa, came to the throne in 1312 and died in 1337. During his reign, the Mandinka began to gain control over Ghana's gold trade, and the empire of Mali overtook that of Ghana.

Mansa Musa oversaw more than conquests and trade. He also had a great influence on architecture in his empire. While on a pilgrimage to Mecca (in present-day Saudi Arabia), he was impressed by the architectural styles he saw, and he brought back an architect to design new Muslim mosques. Although sun-dried mud bricks had long been used for building, Mansa Musa introduced a new building style that combined the mud bricks with timber beams. This style of building made possible the construction of multistory houses.

The Mali Empire was so significant that nations as far off as southern Europe recognized its power. A map of Africa prepared in 1375 by cartographer Abraham Cresques on Majorca (an island off the coast of Spain) depicted the emperor of Mali seated majestically upon a throne while traders from North Africa approached his markets.

# SONGHAY

AROUND THE EIGHTH OR NINTH CENTURY A.D., the Songhay people occupied Gao, the most important city on the Middle Niger River south of Timbuktu, and began to build an empire of their own. In 1464, under the Muslim ruler Sonni Ali, the Songhay began the systematic conquest of their neighbors. They gained possession of Timbuktu and eventually controlled an area from the modern-day nation of Mali to what is now Nigeria. Their holdings included the third major city along the Niger, Jenne, which under the kingdom of Songhay continued to be one of the most important cities in Africa, with a noted university and medical school.

The Songhay civilization was highly organized. Everyone in the kingdom, including slaves, had obligations. Although slavery has never existed without some cruelty, African slaves were often treated as junior members of the community. In 1493, the new emperor, Askia Muhammad, inherited from his predecessor slaves whose obligations were to provide certain goods and services. Blacksmiths had to provide spears, fishermen had to deliver fish or canoes, cattle breeders had to bring in cattle, and others had to perform household services.

# TIMBUKTU

ASKIA MUHAMMAD UPHELD THE TRADITION OF ISLAMIC learning, and during his reign the university of Sankor thrived. Scholars from near and far were allowed to study, teach, and learn in Timbuktu, Gao, and Jenne.

By the late 1400s, the city of Timbuktu reflected the power of the Songhay. Arab travelers of the time described the crowded metropolis, with its markets, mosques, and impressive stone palace, as a resplendent capital of affluence and education.

In 1529, Askia Muhammad, more than eighty years old, was deposed by his son. In 1591, Morocco invaded and conquered the kingdom, effectively ending its influence.

# BENIN

THE KINGDOM OF BENIN WAS located south of Songhay, in the forested delta area of the Niger and Benue Rivers in what is now southern Nigeria. It was established by the Yoruba people. Earlier, those same people had founded Ife, which in Yoruba lore was considered the place of creation, since it was there that Oduduwa, the mythical founder of the Yoruba people, established his throne.

The craftsmen of the ancient city-state of Ife created fine terra-cotta sculptures between the eleventh and fourteenth centuries A.D. Bronze castings of the heads of kings unearthed at the site of Ife in modern times reveal a technology more advanced than that in use in Europe during the same period.

Benin, both the kingdom and the capital city of the same name, emerged in the thirteenth century and peaked in the fifteenth. Like Ife, one of Benin's most important crafts was bronze casting, and some beautiful examples dating to the fifteenth and sixteenth centuries have been found. Benin bronzes could be distributed only by the *oba*, the divine king. Benin was famous as well for its jewelry makers, who worked in gold and ivory.

European traders arrived in Benin in the fifteenth century. Often motivated by the need for spices that would preserve food and enhance its flavor, they soon became more interested in ivory and slaves.

Portuguese traders described the metropolis of Benin as the grandest city in all of western Africa. Its houses were made of red clay polished to such a high luster that it looked like marble. Bronze plaques with scenes commemorating heroic deeds and events in the history of the people of Benin adorned pillars in the square galleries of the palaces.

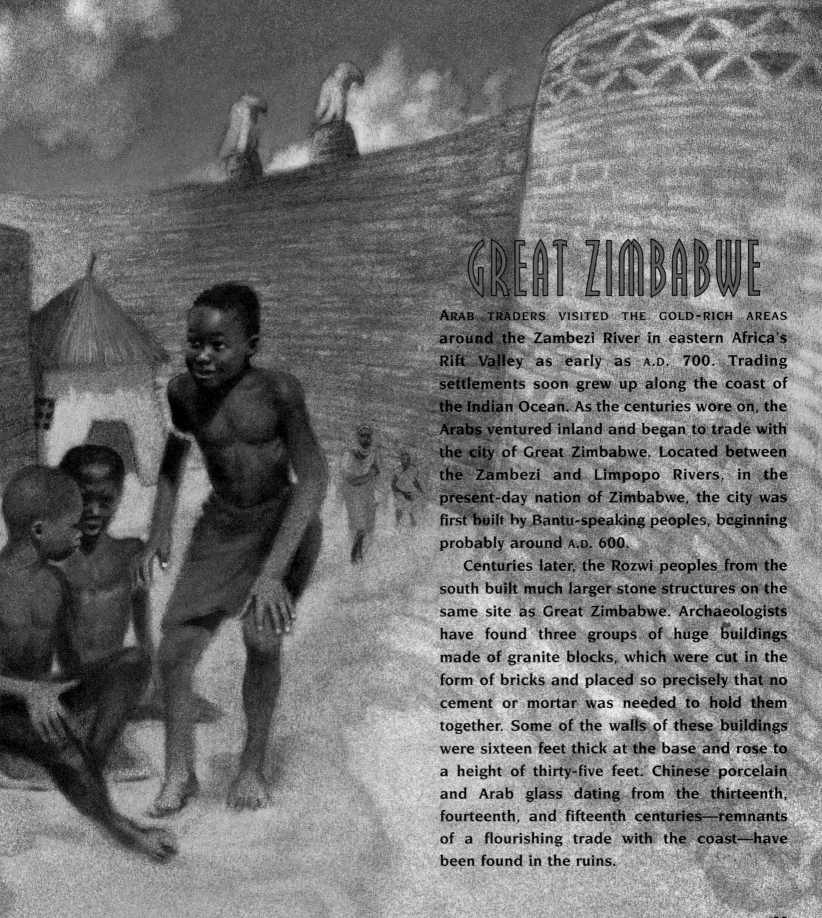

# GREAT ZIMBABWE

ARAB TRADERS VISITED THE GOLD-RICH AREAS around the Zambezi River in eastern Africa's Rift Valley as early as A.D. 700. Trading settlements soon grew up along the coast of the Indian Ocean. As the centuries wore on, the Arabs ventured inland and began to trade with the city of Great Zimbabwe. Located between the Zambezi and Limpopo Rivers, in the present-day nation of Zimbabwe, the city was first built by Bantu-speaking peoples, beginning probably around A.D. 600.

Centuries later, the Rozwi peoples from the south built much larger stone structures on the same site as Great Zimbabwe. Archaeologists have found three groups of huge buildings made of granite blocks, which were cut in the form of bricks and placed so precisely that no cement or mortar was needed to hold them together. Some of the walls of these buildings were sixteen feet thick at the base and rose to a height of thirty-five feet. Chinese porcelain and Arab glass dating from the thirteenth, fourteenth, and fifteenth centuries—remnants of a flourishing trade with the coast—have been found in the ruins.

# KONGO

The empire of the Kongo in central Africa, dating to the fourteenth century, was known for a strong government and excellent craftsmanship. The empire was ruled by the *manikongo*, or king, and was divided into six provinces, each under a governor appointed by the king. Like most other powerful states, Kongo was a trading center. In the 1600s, the enormous amounts of cloth sold through the Kongo—over one hundred thousand yards to Africa alone—were comparable to the amounts sold by major textile-producing cities in Europe.

Kongo began a period of thriving commerce with Europe after Portuguese traders arrived in the 1480s. By 1491, Portuguese craftsmen, missionaries, and soldiers had settled in Mbanza, the capital. Afonso I, who became *manikongo* in 1505, was converted to Christianity by the Portuguese.

Afonso I had wide-reaching power. In 1525, for example, he ordered the seizure of a French ship and crew, declaring that they were sailing along the Kongo coast illegally. Both Afonso and his successor decided to call a temporary halt to the trade in slaves to other parts of Africa and overseas.

In 1641, *manikongo* Garcia II joined forces with the Dutch to control Portuguese slave traders, but the strong empire was ending. Twenty-four years later, Portuguese armies defeated the Kongo rulers and took control of the economy, which then became steadily weaker.

# MUSIC AND DANCE

THE TRADITION OF MUSIC AND DANCE IN Africa has many forms of expression among the different peoples of the continent. Ancient Egyptian paintings show stringed instruments (lyres) and wind instruments made from hollow reeds. Archaeological finds from western Africa include iron double bells, rattles, and xylophones. Benin bronze sculptures depict trumpeters and other musicians. The peoples of western Africa also used drums; the drummers could imitate the pitch and cadence of speech as well as set complex rhythms.

Dancing figures appear in Saharan cliff paintings and on Egyptian monuments. In village life, specific dance patterns were used in different rituals, and the places chosen for such dances were important. Masked figures might have danced individually, but people usually danced, sang, and chanted as a group.

The arts of music and dance still flourish throughout Africa, some forms following ancient traditions and others influenced by contact with other cultures, just as they have always been.

# ART AND RELIGION

LONG BEFORE THE SPREAD OF ISLAM AND Christianity, each of the many different African societies had its own religious system, based on the group's view of the place of humans in nature. Hunting peoples focused on the power of the forest and on spirits of animals; farming peoples on the importance of fertile land and the cycles of the seasons; and herding peoples on strong beliefs in sky-gods. All recognized the power of ancestors and their ties to others in the society. Some societies were guided by special priests; some were led by a ruler who was a sacred figure; some worshiped one god; some, many gods. For all, rituals were a vital part of everyday life.

As part of their worship of nature, gods, and their ancestors, people made rock paintings and fashioned masks, statues, and other objects. Some marked their bodies with dotted lines, spirals, and other shapes—often to indicate the markings of an animal or bird, but always with a special significance. Over the centuries, ritual designs and patterns passed from generation to generation, and the arts flourished and spread through trading networks. Like music and dance, art in its many expressions remains a vital part of African culture.

# EUROPEAN TRADE

BY THE MID-1400S, EUROPEAN TRADE with the African kingdoms was thriving. Led by the Portuguese, Europeans traveled down the west coast of Africa to trade for the riches they found there. Exactly what riches the Europeans sought can be told from the names the Portuguese gave to the regions where they traded.

The Grain Coast, now Liberia, was a fertile agricultural area yielding corn, rice, and other grains. The name, however, does not refer to these grains but to a kind of sweet pepper called *malaguetta*, which means "grains of paradise." This pepper was much sought after in Europe as a seasoning for food.

Below the Grain Coast was the area still called the Ivory Coast, where abundant elephant herds yielded ivory tusks valued all over the world for jewelry and other ornaments. Below the Ivory Coast was the Gold Coast, in the area of present-day Ghana. For two centuries after the Portuguese arrived, in 1471, the Gold Coast was Africa's center of trade with Europe.

A fourth coast was to become an even greater center for trade—the Slave Coast (in present-day Nigeria). Although the name Slave Coast is applied to this one section, slavery became the main trading attraction all along the four-thousand-mile Atlantic coast. To build their colonies and exploit the riches of the New World, the Portuguese and other Europeans took millions of strong young Africans from their homelands.

# SLAVERY AND COLONIZATION

SLAVERY HAD LONG EXISTED IN AFRICA, AND A SLAVE TRADE WITH THE ARABS TO THE NORTH HAD BEEN conducted for centuries. Thus, when the Portuguese began taking slaves out of Africa in the 1400s, the African rulers with whom they traded had no objection. In fact, during the years of the organized European slave trade with Africa—from about 1500 to the 1880s, with its peak between 1750 and 1800—many African rulers and entire kingdoms devoted most of their energies to trading in human lives.

In Africa, however, slaves had rights as well as responsibilities. New World slavery was chattel slavery, in which slaves were regarded as property, not people, and had no rights at all. It was a brutal system in which millions died, either on their way to the New World or after they arrived there. During the Middle Passage—the voyage across the Atlantic Ocean—many of the captives committed suicide by jumping overboard or starving themselves rather than be taken to an unknown land and fate. Many more died from the harsh and inhuman conditions on the ships, where they were packed suffocatingly tight into the holds and allowed little fresh air or exercise.

Equally great suffering awaited them in the New World, where they were forced to clear forests, dig canals, plant fields, build towns and cities, mine ore and forge iron, raise and shear sheep and weave cloth, tame horses and drive cattle, and care for whole families who were not their own, cooking food and doing laundry, soothing crying babies, healing illnesses, and digging graves—all with little hope of ever escaping their condition.

Not only the slaves themselves suffered. Western Africa as a whole also suffered. Since European traders were eager for Africa's natural resources, economies in Africa became focused on giving up those resources rather than enhancing them through conservation and manufacturing. So many European goods arrived in payment for natural resources and slaves that many African craftsmen, including textile workers and metal processors, stopped making their special products, and many traditions were disrupted. Most important, western Africa suffered from the loss of millions of its youngest, strongest, and healthiest people. Instead of contributing their skills and strengths and intelligence to their homelands, they were forced to use them in the New World.

Yet more sorrow was in store for Africa. Beginning in the late nineteenth century, various European nations colonized the ancient lands, further exploiting the natural resources and the labor of the people. Between 1880 and 1912, all of Africa except Ethiopia and Liberia (colonized by ex-slaves from the United States) fell under the control of European powers. But the peoples of Africa retained their spirit, their strength, and their pride in traditions, and beginning in the early 1950s they threw off the colonial yoke and formed new and independent nations.

So, too, the Africans forcibly taken from their homelands retained their spirit and pride. No one could take their traditions from them, and over the centuries their cultures became part of New World cultures. North, Central, and South American, Caribbean, and West Indian language and literature, music and dance, religion and folklore were all enriched by the influence of slaves. In this way, their African beginnings, though far away and long ago, could never be forgotten.

# MILESTONES IN AFRICAN HISTORY

(MOST DATES ARE APPROXIMATE)

**100,000 B.C.** First *Homo sapiens*, Olduvai Gorge

**35,000** Rudimentary counting devices, South Africa

**24,000** First rock paintings in Africa, Namibia

**7500** Fishing communities in southern Sahara

**6000** Cattle domesticated, Sahara

**5000** Grain farming, Egypt

**3800** Nubian culture begins

**3100** Egypt unifies and system of divine kingship begins

**3000** Egyptians develop writing system

**2650** First Egyptian pyramids built

**2550** Pharaoh Khufu (Cheops) begins pyramids at Giza

**750–650** Kushite kings rule Egypt

**600** Camels introduced to Egypt by Assyrian or Persian invaders

**500** In Nigeria, Nok culture develops; it is to flourish for a thousand years and be the source of the first ironworking in sub-Saharan Africa

**250** Settlement of Jenne-jeno founded as a small farming village

**180** Alphabetic writing appears in Meroë

**100** Meroë, a great industrial center in which iron technology flourishes, at height of power

**51–30** Cleopatra rules Egypt

**A.D. 300–700** Axum (northeastern Ethiopia) a major trading center where gold and bronze coins are minted

**350** Axum conquers Meroë and Christianity is introduced to region

**450–1230** Ghana gold trade flourishes

**600s** Arab traders begin to travel south across the Sahara

**600–700** Bantu-speaking peoples build city of Great Zimbabwe

**800** Rise of West African kingdom of Ghana

**800–1000** Jenne-jeno at height of power

**900** Great Zimbabwe becomes a major power

**1000** Empire of Ghana at its peak, controlling Atlantic ports and trade routes across the Sahara

**1200s** Mandinka people succeed Ghanian rulers

**1240** Sundiata Keita of the kingdom of Kangaba establishes the new empire of Mali, ending the kingdom of Ghana

**1300** Empire of Benin becomes famed for its trade wealth and bronzeworking

**1312–1337** Mansa Musa, Sundiata's grandson, rules Mali and leads his people to convert to Islam; Timbuktu becomes a center of Islamic scholarship

**1324** Mansa Musa travels to Mecca, bringing so much gold with him that there is inflation in the region for many years to come

**1340** Empire of Songhay founded

**1440** Portuguese traders begin taking slaves out of Africa

**1464** Muslim ruler Sonni Ali becomes ruler of Songhay, formerly a province of Mali, and it begins to flourish as a separate empire

**1480–1490** Kingdom of Kongo begins time of significant trade with Portugal

**1493** Songhay empire reaches its greatest height under Askia Muhammad; during his reign, Leo Africanus (a Muslim from Spain) visits Timbuktu and writes that "manuscripts and books are sold for more money than any other merchandise"

**late 1400s** Monomatopan Confederacy ends; Rozwi Confederacy founded; Timbuktu at its height

**1500–1880s** European slave trade with Africa expands to include English, Dutch, and French as well as Portuguese

**1525–1600** Afonso I, ruler of Kongo, controls trade with Europeans and temporarily halts slave trade

**1591** Songhay defeated in Battle of Tondibi; Moroccan occupation lasts until 1618

**1665** Portuguese armies defeat Kongo rulers

**1750–1800** Peak of African slave trade

# BIBLIOGRAPHY

Davidson, Basil. *Africa in History*. Revised and expanded edition. New York: Collier Books, 1991.

———. *African Civilization Revisited: From Antiquity to Modern Times*. Trenton, NJ: Africa World Press, 1991.

———. *The Lost Cities of Africa*. Revised edition. Boston: Little, Brown, 1987.

Everett, Susanne. *History of Slavery*. Secaucus, NJ: Chartwell Books, 1991.

Mazrui, Ali A. *The Africans*. Boston: Little, Brown, 1986.

Oliver, Roland. *The African Experience: Major Themes in African History from Earliest Times to the Present*. New York: HarperCollins, 1992.

Oliver, Roland, and Anthony Atmore. *The African Middle Ages: 1400–1800*. New York: Cambridge University Press, 1989.

Oliver, Roland, and Brian M. Fagan. *Africa in the Iron Age c. 500 B.C. to A.D. 1400*. New York: Cambridge University Press, 1990.

Scarre, Chris. *Smithsonian Timelines of the Ancient World*. New York: Dorling Kindersley, 1993.

Snowden, Frank M., Jr. *Before Color Prejudice: The Ancient View of Blacks*. Cambridge, MA: Harvard University Press, 1991.

## ESPECIALLY FOR YOUNG PEOPLE

Bellerophon staff. *Ancient Africa*. 2 vols. Santa Barbara, CA: Bellerophon Books, 1992–93.

Boyd, Herbert. *African History for Beginners. Part I: African Dawn—A Diasporan View*. New York: Writers and Readers, 1991.

Haskins, James. *Count Your Way Through Africa*. Minneapolis, MN: Carolrhoda Books, 1989.

Haskins, Jim, and Joann Biondi. *From Afar to Zulu: A Dictionary of African Cultures*. New York: Walker, 1995.

Jones, Constance. *Africa, 1500–1900*. New York: Facts on File, 1993.

Mann, Kenny. *Monomatapa, Great Zimbabwe, Zululand, Lesotho: Southern Africa*. Englewood Cliffs, NJ: Silver Burdett, 1996.

McKissack, Patricia C., and Fredrick L. McKissack. *The Royal Kingdoms of Ghana, Mali, and Songhay: Life in Medieval Africa*. New York: Henry Holt, 1995.

Musgrove, Margaret. *Ashanti to Zulu: African Traditions*. New York: Puffin Books, 1992.

47

# INDEX